Shattered Yet Gathered

By: *Yesenia "Patti" Pena*

Shattered Yet Gathered

Published by Dreamers Arise, LLC

Houston, Texas 77379

A division of First Fruits Christian Center

Email: dreamersarisellc@gmail.com

Unless otherwise noted, all scripture references are taken from the King James Version of the Bible.

© Copyright 2020

ISBN- 978-0-578-69650-8

All rights reserved. No part of this book may be reproduced or used in any manner whatsoever, without the express written permission of the publisher, except for the use of brief quotations in a book review.

Printed in the United States of America

First Printing, 2020

Table Of Contents

Dedication

Special Thanks

Introduction

Chapter 1	Daddy's Girl
Chapter 2	So Hard to Say Goodbye
Chapter 3	Trying to Find my Way
Chapter 4	The Downward Spiral
Chapter 5	Turnaround is Here
Chapter 6	The Beginning in Christ
Chapter 7	The Breakup
Chapter 8	The Prophecy
Chapter 9	The Big Comeback
Chapter 10	I Know Who I Am

Dedication

I dedicate this book first and foremost to my two beautiful daughters.

This book is also dedicated to those who have lost hope, experienced brokenness in childhood, or as an adult.

I dedicate it to the outcasts, rejected and hurting.

May you find hope, inspiration, answers, and a drive to push forward to believe God for the impossible.

May this book give you wings to be set free, dream bigger, and aspire you to move past your pain to your God given purpose.

God wants to take the shattered pieces of your life and share them with the multitudes, so open your heart and mind to God.

Get honest with yourself right where you are so God can begin to heal you and take you to the next level in your walk with Him.

May God bless you richly
Your servant
"Patti"

Special Thanks

I want to thank first and foremost my Pastors Juan and Ruthy Martinez. Both of you have always seen me through the eyes of grace. I have experienced the love of Jesus through your pastoral guidance. This has set me free in so many ways. A million thank you's from the bottom of my heart.

To Pastors Silvestre and Molly for seeing the greatness in me and speaking life into my destiny. Your words have helped me see beyond my limitations. I am forever grateful to God for the both of you.

Pastors Luis and Josie for your great love for me. You two have always treated me like family. I have always felt so welcome when I minister at your church.

Special thanks to Henry and Liz for pushing me to release this book I wrote two years ago. God has used the both of you to fulfill my calling as an author.

I am forever grateful to everyone who contributed to the publishing of this book. I am blessed beyond belief that so many of you believe in the God who lives inside of me. This book would not have been possible without your faithful gifts.

Lastly, I am forever grateful to my Lord and Savior Jesus Christ for working through me to write this book. Thank You Jesus, for your great love and plan for my life. May your mission for the release of this book be accomplished on earth as it is in heaven.

Introduction

Where do I begin? The real question here is, how could I be called to write a book? Feeling so unqualified to be called an author, this was another name given to me as I grew more in Christ. The Lord has a way of calling you into roles you have not yet embraced or stepped into. Where do I start? Should I be myself and just write, or do I study other writers? All I know how to be is me, so Holy Spirit USE ME, TAKE OVER MY MIND, MY HANDS AS I TYPE AND SPEAK through Me LORD. You know who will read this book and what they need to hear.

In Jesus' Name, Amen

1

Daddy's Girl

Growing up, I was not brought up in a Christian home. I did not know there was a God that loved me, a God who has a plan for my life. I remember a Spanish Holy Spirit filled Pentecostal church we would walk to at the corner of my street. The music was beautiful, and I had many friends there. My mother said it was my happy place. She recalls combing my hair and dressing me up for church and how excited I was to go to the house of God. I was only 5 years old, but I remember thinking the drummer was kind of cute. (lol) I also remember my mother being in the women's ministry. I was brought up with both of my parents. However, I don't recall my father ever going to church with us. We even took a family picture at church, but my father wasn't in the picture. In fact, every professional family picture we took didn't include my father. We went to that church about a year.

I was a daddy's girl. When my Dad was home, I felt protected and free. My Dad would spoil my siblings and me so much. He was a happy person, great father, and provider He always found ways of showing us how much he loved us. When we were young, he would let us jump on his back and ride him all around the house. One of my favorite memories was when my Dad would come home from out of town with a huge watermelon. My family would gather around the table and eat the whole thing. I have five siblings, two sisters and three brothers so eating a whole watermelon was not a hard thing to do. Our dad would often take us to fun places too. He and my mother would make sure we had big birthday parties. When I turned 13 my Dad gave me a diamond and I had a huge party to celebrate at my house. My Dad loved to hear me sing. He was so proud of me when I won 2nd place singing "Como La Flor" by Selena. My passion to sing came from my dad, he was a great singer. When my Dad would come home from work my sister Erika and I would take off his boots and massage his feet. We really loved him.

Around that time, my mother's father was very sick in the hospital and my grandfather was very dear to her heart. I remember watching my mother pray for her father to be healed. She really believed that God would heal him completely. When my grandfather passed away my mother was devastated. She became angry with God, and she stopped going to church. She would only send us to church. The church was later burned down by young boys in my neighborhood that didn't have anything better to do. That's when I stopped going to church too. I was too young to understand who God truly was. I remember my father buying us books that taught us stories about the bible. I would read those books and be in awe of the pictures of Jonah and the whale, Moses stretching out his rod while God parted the Red Sea. Yet, God seemed too far away to me. My father worked at a major grocery chain as a Butcher. He later became a Meat Department Manager. However, after 20 years of working there, the grocery chain forced him to retire. My Mother also worked at the same grocery chain as a Cashier. That's where she met my father. After they retired my father, my mother says my father was approached by one of his friends to begin selling drugs. Since my father was genuinely nice and sought his friends' approval, he turned to drug dealing. However, my father never allowed his personal life to invade our home. So, we only remember how awesome and loving our father was.

As the years went by, my mother's anger grew even stronger. In my household, we only spoke Spanish, so when I started school, I didn't know any English.

In the first grade, reading seemed so difficult for me because I couldn't read English, so the teacher flunked me. My mother's anger became enraged towards me. She couldn't believe I had failed the first grade. The whole summer she abused me mentally and physically. She told me every day how stupid I was for failing the first grade. I felt so hopeless and the devil made sure fear crippled my thinking. I never wanted to fail another grade again. I never wanted to disappoint my mother again. So, I became an honor roll student and was placed in advanced classes. I was afraid to ever fail another grade and my mother's mental/physical abuse scarred me for years.

My mother's abusive ways landed her in jail and my older brother was taken into CPS custody since she lost control in her anger and left bruises all over him.

I still remember that morning hearing my brother pleading for his life as my mother lost control. I was so scared. He ran to school not knowing where else to turn and the school reported the abuse. My big brother was very protective of us even though sometimes he was a bully. He would always teach us how to fight and throw us into the pool in the deep end. He would then rescue us if he thought we were drowning. It was so important to him that we could fight and take care of ourselves. He wanted us to be tough. Yet I wasn't much of a fighter. My siblings would make fun of me because I didn't want to fight. I would cry but there was no time to seem weak around them.

We never knew when my mother would lose it. We thought for sure my mother would stop abusing us after she went to jail, but you can't go to prison for mental abuse. My household was always chaotic. There was no peace in my home. My older brother would make us fight each other because he wanted us to be tough.

We had a beautiful home it was the most beautiful house in the neighborhood. Much later, I discovered why my father was hardly home because he was a drug dealer and went out of town a lot. We had nice clothes, we had gold rings on each finger, and we went to many places together as a family. Looking from the outside in we looked like the perfect Mexican Brady Bunch family. I have no doubt that my mother and my father loved us. Yet my Mother's childhood was very abusive. She grew up being abused as well. So, she repeated the cycle with us.

In the summertime, my sister and I would be sent to my grandparent's house in Rio Grande Valley, Texas. We would love to go there because my grandfather was a farmer. He had a huge yard filled with apples, oranges, lemons, mangos, and the list goes on. We would run in the field and makeup dances with our friends. One summer, I went with my grandmother to visit my aunt in Santa Rosalio, Mexico. They had a huge ranch filled with cows and horses. I loved to play outside all by myself. One day when I was about to go play outside, a huge rattlesnake met me at the door with his huge teeth claws ready to bite me. Thank God my uncle was right behind me, so he chopped off the snake's head with his huge long knife. My uncle was used to killing snakes and later that evening he showed me the length of the snake. It was a very long snake. I was too scared to ever go back outside and play at the ranch again. Little did I know God would speak to me later about the meaning of this event later in life.

SUMMARY

1 CORINTHIANS 15:33 says "Bad Company Corrupts Good Character." In Chapter 1, we learn that who we surround ourselves with plays a major role in our decisions. Just as my father was pursued by his peers to sell drugs, so we too can be pursued to sin against God if we allow bad company to corrupt our Godly ways. In Genesis 4:7God tells Cain "If you do well, will not your countenance be lifted up? And if you do not do well, sin is crouching at the door; and its desire is for you, but you must

master it." Cain was so jealous of Abel that his sin mastered him, and he killed his own brother. My mother is another example, if we don't learn how to master our sin that very same sin will end up mastering us. We must pay attention to the sin that so easily ensnares us and master it through prayer and God's presence.

QUESTIONS – Chapter 1

1. Were you brought up in an abusive home? If so, how have you dealt with the pain?

2. Have you forgiven those who have hurt you? If not, what is holding you back from forgiving them?

3. Did you find yourself repeating the same abusive cycles? Are you still repeating those cycles, or have you been set free from them?

4. How has your childhood affected you now?

5. How has God helped you let go of the pain and past?

2

So Hard to Say Goodbye

I believe our childhood affects us more than we know. And if we don't deal with our issues, then we become the issue. The question then becomes, how do we deal with our issues if we don't know how? I had no idea I had issues. No really, I had no idea. Everyone around me dealt with some level of dysfunction. I was just a young girl shaped by my circumstances and crippled by fear. By the age of 12 years old, I thought I was in love. Falling in love was my escape from everything. I was looking for love and lust was looking for me. I thought love was a fairytale. I thought if I fell in love my prince charming would come and rescue me. Once I was rescued then everything would be okay.

By the age of 14, I went to go live with my boyfriend for 3 months, only to beg my parents to let me come back home. I thought I knew it all, but I didn't know anything about life. I was even more miserable living with my boyfriend. All we did was fight. There was no peace there. I couldn't wait to go back home. Although my father let me come back home, he didn't treat me the same again. He didn't see me as his little girl anymore. I was a disgrace to him because I left the house to go live with my boyfriend. I felt the distance between us, and it was hard to deal with. Once I returned home, it was different, and I no longer felt like the young girl who left although that's all I was. I felt the rejection from my father, and I didn't know how to face him. I went back to my old school but by then, the same spirit of anger that controlled my mother begin to wrap itself around me. I was angry all the time for no reason, so I found my escape by getting high. Marijuana was my drug of choice, because it would make me laugh until I couldn't laugh anymore. I was still out of control skipping school, fighting, and getting high. I even got kicked out of school and was placed in the guidance center because I couldn't stop fighting and skipping school.

My sister was in juvenile by this time, so my father and I would go visit her often. One day, while we were visiting her, a guy who was also in juvenile with my sister approached me. We said hi to one another and later he asked my sister if he could write to me. She gave him our home address and we began to write to each other. When he got out of juvenile we started dating. I didn't know it then, but he would later become the father of my two daughters. One day, while I was at his house, I began to have knots in my stomach. I knew something was wrong back at home. I called my house various times and the line was continuously busy. My parents never came to pick me up, so I ended up spending the night at my boyfriend's house.

Early the next morning, my older brother came to pick me up. When I got in the car my brother told me that my father was in the hospital in critical condition. He didn't want to tell me that my father had been murdered. He drove me to our house and there were private investigators and family members from Mexico at my house already. Everyone approached me with a hug and tears in their eyes. I was the last one to find out my father had been killed. I saw the bullet holes in the kitchen walls and blood everywhere in the room where my father was murdered. I remember running to my room and hugging my sister. All I could do was cry. I was so shocked and angry.

A group of hitmen had been hired to kill my father, so they watched our home. They watched my brothers, my sister, and I leave the house one by one. My mother was having a garage sale that day so, the gates to our home were wide open and so was our entrance door. My father was resting watching television as my mother massaged his head when a group of hitmen came into our house with SWAT team vests on. They disconnected our phone lines and tortured my father with crowbars. They took my mother to the other rooms in the house and made her empty out every closet. My mom, my youngest sister, two of my cousins, and my youngest brother were there when all this happened. They were looking for drugs and money. Little did they know that my father was trying to stop selling drugs.

My father and my sister had made a pact to leave drugs alone while she was in juvenile. So, my father didn't have any drugs anymore in our home. They thought my father was lying so they put a gun to my mother's head threatening to kill her. By this time, my father's hands were broken, and his head was filled with blood running down to his entire body. He had little strength left due to the beating he endured with the crowbars. They broke many bones in his body. However, with the little strength my father had left he pushed those men out of my mom's way, and they shot him 6 times until he was dead. They ran out of the house shooting at my mom as she ran after them to shut the door so they wouldn't come back in. Not one bullet hit my mother. As they disappeared, my mother ran outside looking for help since our neighbors were paramedics, so they rushed to my father, but my father was already pronounced dead. My little cousin says she saw my father before he took his last breath and she could hear him say "Mis Hijos, Mis Hijos" (my children, my children). My father died not knowing if everyone had been murdered. This changed our lives forever.

SUMMARY

Romans 8:1 says "Therefore, there is now no condemnation to those who are in CHRIST JESUS." In my story, I felt condemned because I didn't know Christ when I left home to go live with my boyfriend; however, when we sin once we're in Christ, condemnation no longer has a right to rule over us.

We are convicted not condemned. Christ has paid for all our sins at Calvary. Galatians 6:8 says, "Those who sow to the flesh will reap destruction." My father paid for his sin with his life. He lost his life over it. There are many things we too can lose if we choose to continue in sin. We must sow to the spirit to reap abundant life.

QUESTIONS – Chapter 2

1. Is there an event that took place in your life that changed you forever?

2. Do you still ask God why did that have to happen, or do you understand now why things happened that way?

3. Have you made peace with the pain or do you find yourself still angry?

4. Do you know that your pain is your purpose and if so, have you shared your story with someone to help them with their pain?

3

Trying to Find My Way

After my father's death, we moved to a new home and school district. Everything in our lives as we knew it had changed. We all were trying to find ways to cope with our loss. I continued in the relationship with the guy I met from juvenile. Deep down inside I knew that relationship wasn't good for me, but somehow it seemed to provide an escape from the pain. At this point, I was ready to try almost anything to numb the pain.

Life became even more difficult because we didn't have any money. My mother hadn't worked in years, so we lived off survival benefits from my father's social security earnings. We were used to nice clothes, shoes, and jewelry, but when my father passed away my mom had to make ends meet on a limited budget. I still wanted to maintain the lifestyle of dressing nice, so I started to shoplift. I would steal clothes and makeup from the mall until I got caught. I still didn't take school seriously, so I would skip school and go to my boyfriend's house. My life was spiraling out of control.

At the age of 16, I ended up getting pregnant. I decided to move in with my boyfriend thinking everything would be peaches and cream. How naïve I was! He became very abusive and was hardly ever home. I spent most of my pregnancy alone in his room. There were nights when I would call out to my father and be in tears. I missed my father so much! I felt so alone and trapped in my pregnant body. I didn't have any friends because they were all in high school getting their education while I was in a room pregnant. I didn't know much about God, but I would always look outside of my boyfriend's bedroom window and stare at the sky. I know now God was with me through it all. I gave birth to my first daughter Cassandra on 12/14/1996. That was one of the happiest days of my life. I loved my little girl. She had so much hair and she had a very fair complexion. I remember staring at her as she slept and her holding my fingers to ensure I was there next to her.

The abuse with my daughter's father continued. We had no respect for each other anymore. All I wanted was to get a job to get my own place and get away from him. My friend at the time began speaking to me about becoming an exotic dancer. She had her own place, a vehicle and was able to support her entire family. I was desperate for my own independence, so I took her up on the offer. I never wanted to face the reality that I was an exotic dancer, so I would numb my shame through alcohol. I would drink until I could get the courage to go on stage and approach customers. I still remember my first time on stage. I was so scared. Customers would always tell me that I didn't look like I belonged there. I only worked on the weekends, but I made enough money to get a vehicle and my own place. That lifestyle led me to start going to clubs and drinking all the time. I couldn't see myself having fun without alcohol. I found an excuse to drink for everything. All I wanted to do was numb the pain of yesterday. I didn't dance for a long period because I was offered a job at a rent to own company as a Customer Service Rep; however, that didn't stop me from drinking. Even though I got a regular job, I missed the money I made in the clubs. I struggled to make ends meet.

My relationship with my mother was still broken and so was the relationship with my daughter's father. We loved each other very much but we didn't know how to heal from the pain we caused each other over the years. Our trust had been broken and so had our hope. I continued to search for love in all the wrong places. I remember saying "there's got to be more to life than this." Well little did I know that there was.

SUMMARY

Psalm 147:3 says, " He heals the brokenhearted and binds up their wounds." This verse tells us plainly that God is our Healer. No man or woman can heal us only God. God is the only one who has the power to go into our soul and heart to heal us.

Joshua 1:8 says, "On this book of the law you should meditate on day and night so you can prosper in all that you do." Success comes from God. Our job is to stay IN CHRIST and not allow distractions to keep us from the greater that God is trying to do in our lives. We must meditate on God's word until it comes alive to us on the inside and it causes us to say "there's got to be more to life than this" because the truth is......there is!

QUESTIONS – Chapter 3

1. Have you tolerated an abusive relationship because of the way you were brought up that dysfunction became normal?

2. Can you recall a time when you used a substance or created a bad habit to heal your pain?

3. Have you gotten used to a certain lifestyle that you find yourself doing anything to maintain it including sinning against God?

4. Have you loved someone so much, but you didn't know how to mend the brokenness between you?

4

The Downward Spiral

I continued to get high, party and drink. This had become the story of my life. I was broken and empty. My fears and distrust made me close off my heart from everyone. I didn't know how to love including those closest to me. My heart had grown cold from all the abuse I encountered, and I became very selfish. I intentionally hurt others before they ever thought about hurting me. The distrust I had towards men caused me to become very mean towards them. All I wanted to do was hang out with my friends.

My oldest daughter got neglected along the way because I didn't know how to be a mother. I was too selfish and caught up in my own pain to put her first. I loved my daughter, but my issues had overpowered me, I would leave her at her grandmother's or a friend's house so I could go party. I only cared about having fun and enjoying my life. My behavior affected my daughter in many ways. She started to resent me, and she didn't want a relationship with me. Later, when I started to change, no matter how much I apologized it was never enough. She constantly reminded me that I wasn't there for her as a Mom. I started to see the same anger that plagued my mother, and me try to attach itself to her. Again, I loved my daughter, but I was so blinded by my own strongholds that I had no power to say no to anything that enticed my flesh.

My flesh was ruling me and telling me what to do and who to be. I was conformed to this world without heavenly convictions or perspectives. I had adapted to my dysfunction so completely it was normal to me. It was all I ever knew in my little world. Everyone around me drank, smoked, and went to clubs.

I was drowning in the pain of yesterday, trying to find some relief through alcohol, men, and drugs.

I remember going to a club one night and getting jumped by 8 girls, who broke all the windows to my car. They jumped me because I had a confrontation with one of them weeks before over an ex-boyfriend. When they saw me at the club alone that night, they decided to jump on me. I was living with my brother at the time, and my life was spiraling dangerously out of control. I remember getting so drunk that I would be in the toilet the next day in tears and throwing up because the hangovers were so heavy. I would promise myself that I would never ever touch liquor again. Little did I know than that I could never change in my own strength, so the cycle just continued. God began to speak to me in dreams showing me the life I was living was leading me down a path of destruction. I would have dreams of the bars burning up in flames. Each time I went to the club things got worse for me, but it was the only lifestyle I knew. There was no real pleasure in what I did. It was all a vicious cycle. The same music, same people, same hangover, same story. My soul kept screaming, "There has got to be more to life than this."

SUMMARY

John 4 says "JESUS is the fountain of living water that never runs dry." Everything else will leave you thirsty again. (Luke 8:43-48)

The woman in the bible with the issue of blood ran to various physicians but no one could heal her only God. She wasted time and money looking for a solution outside of God. We must understand that turning to substances and people will never heal the pain from the past. They will only be a bandage to our wounds. (Psalm 143:7) Jesus says he has come to heal the broken hearted and deliver those who are oppressed in spirit. Only Jesus has the power to heal us and is larger than life.

QUESTIONS - Chapter 4
1. Have you ever been stuck in a pattern you couldn't break out of? Are you still in that pattern? What did you do or what are you trying to do to break free from the patterns that damage? (Romans 12:1-2)

2. Have you hurt your children along the way because of your selfish ways and bad habits? What have you done to fix your relationship with your children? Or do you still battle with selfishness?

3. Has your soul ever cried out "there's got to be more to life than this?" If so, have your discovered that God is larger than life?

4. Has your hurt and pain led you to turn to other substances or people for relief?

5. Do you feel like your world is falling apart? If so, is it by your own choices or God breaking you to draw you closer to him?

5

Turnaround is Here

When I turned 23 years old, one of my long-time friends I used to party with gave her life to Jesus. We met at the club and became partying and drinking buddies. She never talked much about how she grew up. I do know that she found herself in a very unhealthy relationship. She had hit rock bottom and started going to church. Her family always prayed for her even when she was lost. She came from a Christian family and they all actively attended church.

We had lost contact, but she called me one day and told me she had started attending church. I thought she had lost her mind (lol). Her conversation, her attitude, she was so full of joy and peace. She would talk to me about how beautiful life looked to her now. She would tell me how green the trees were and how blue the sky was to her. She was truly high off Jesus, and I was still high on marijuana! Lol.

She would invite me to church every weekend and I would not go. One Sunday morning, I got up and just joined her to church. She was so surprised and happy that I joined her. I loved the worship songs, but honestly, I had not encountered Jesus. I didn't understand why my friend was so happy and I was so empty. I wanted what she had, but I didn't know how to tap into that joy. When I saw my friend again it was an answer for me, a solution, and a way out. The peace and joy she walked in opened a longing in me I can't describe. I just knew I had to have it.

You see, I was running from facing my own brokenness. Until I saw my friend, I didn't realize how broken and wounded I was. I didn't know there was a Savior waiting to heal and deliver me from all my pain. I felt I always had to defend myself. I wanted to make sure no one ever hurt me again. I wore anger like a garment to protect me from everything. My friend showed me that I could take all my fears, heartache, and pain to the feet of Jesus and leave it.

One night, we watched a video called, "The Spirit of Python" by Jenzeten Franklin. That video changed my life forever. I saw how the spirit of python had wrapped itself around me and was sucking life out of me. I learned that the python spirit is assigned to us to take the joy and abundant life Christ died for away. That's why I couldn't see or enjoy life the way my friend was able to. The python spirit tries to keep you in bondage to the world with a dysfunctional lifestyle. It keeps you entangled and entertained with the worlds system of happiness which is no joy at all.

What it offers at best is temporary fun and fulfillment that leaves you empty and desolate time after time.

I remember going back to church and running to the altar giving God everything. That day at the altar, I experienced an encounter with the presence of God that brought so much peace and life to my soul. It birthed a desire in me to want to know God and read everything in His Word. I wanted to continue to feel His Presence and tell everyone about God. I was never the same again. I no longer wanted to get high, drink or go to clubs. All I wanted to do was go to church and hang around those that had a relationship with Him as I now did. It made me grateful for the price JESUS paid on the cross. I wanted to serve

Him. While on that altar, He softened my heart and took away a lot of my anger. I made a list of people I needed to ask for forgiveness, and they forgave me. I also forgave my Mother and asked for her forgiveness. That experience took away a lot of the pride I walked in and made me humbler. All I wanted to do was please God and live for Him.

I became so zealous to learn God's word that I started having bible studies at my apartment. I had so many questions about the bible, so when the bible was being taught, I was like a sponge soaking up everything that was being taught to me. I fell in love with God's word. I would read the bible for hours. I had finally found what I had been looking for all along,

God who is larger than life. I became an evangelist at heart even though I had no idea what an evangelist was at the time. I just wanted to tell everyone about Jesus. My friend and I would go on the streets and talk to anyone we saw about Jesus and we would pray for them. I found such fulfillment in praying for people and talking to them about Jesus. My love for Jesus grew stronger by the day.

However, Satan was not going to give me up that easily. Afterall, I served him for years, so he knew exactly what to do to keep me from giving God everything. He knew my weakness and sin patterns. Although I had let go of drinking and partying, I was still fornicating with my daughter's father. I began to feel so convicted for sleeping with him that I would cry afterwards. He thought I was crazy, yet I didn't know how to stop. I begged God one day to take him out of my life or to change him. Months later, he ended up in prison.

SUMMARY

(Read John 10:10): JESUS came to give us life to the fullest and If we are not experiencing the abundant life that HE died on the cross for us to have. Then it's time we ask God to allow us to have a true encounter with HIM that will change your life forever. (John 15:4-6) JESÚS said if we abide (hide/stay connected) in HIM that we shall bear much fruit meaning we shall do and see great things in this life. LIFE BEGINS with JESUS. (John 14:6) HE IS THE WAY, THE TRUTH AND THE LIFE. There is no way we will ever enjoy life on our own. We may have temporary happiness, BUT true joy only comes from Jesus. This joy has a name and His name is Jesus!

QUESTIONS – Chapter 5

1. Have you gone to church and saw others be so full of joy, peace, life, and purpose yet you can't seem to tap into that experience with JESUS?

2. What do you believe is holding you back from giving JESUS your everything? Is it a lie you have bought into? If so, what lies do you think you have bought into?

3. Are you in a habitual sin you can't seem to break free from? Have you asked God to intervene?

4. Have you had a true encounter with JESUS? What was it like? If not, have you asked God to allow you to encounter Him?

6

The Beginning in Christ

I continued to grow in God's word and go to church. I started volunteering in prison ministry and the children's ministry. I was even a prayer partner at my church. I also joined the praise team and sang. My friend who led me to Christ always says that she knows there's a God because every time she saw me singing on the praise team it reminded her that God truly is mighty to save. If anyone knew how much of a mess I was, it was her (lol).

I loved going to church. I never missed a Sunday or a Wednesday night bible study. My pastor at the time had committed adultery and many left that church. He stepped down from his pastoral position and started counseling. He wrote an apology letter and read it to the church his last Sunday there. I never saw him again. I was a baby Christian, and I remember being very confused, disappointed, and hurt. It made me feel sorry for his wife and family. I didn't understand why a Pastor would do that. After all, I thought all men in church were perfect! lol. Looking back, it affected me and made it difficult for me to respect leadership. It was hard to receive from those in authority over me. My trust had been broken.

Most of us at that church left including my friend that led me to Christ. One of my friends took me to visit a different church that was under my church covering to listen to another pastor. When I went to that new church I felt right at home, and I started attending there. I also got involved right away in children's ministry, the praise team and being a prayer partner.

By this time, my oldest daughter started asking for her father who was in prison. So, I took her to go see him in prison and all he talked about was JESUS. He asked me to give him another chance and said he had found JESUS. I believed him since I knew God had changed me. So, I believed God had changed him too although I didn't have 100% peace about it. When he got out of prison, we got married and I got pregnant a year and a half later with our second daughter.

The problems in our marriage began to increase when I got pregnant. I felt so hopeless because he always threw my past in my face although I had truly changed. He couldn't see the new Patti and he held on to the past pain I caused him although, I had forgiven him for the past pain he caused me. Here I was once again pregnant, and my marriage was not working out. I was so downcast because he had left the house with another woman for a month and a half before my delivery date. I continued to go to church and cling to JESUS. HE was my only comfort. Every time I would open the bible somehow the pages would always turn to "ISAIAH 54:4 FOR THE LORD YOUR MAKER IS YOUR HUSBAND." I had no idea God was calling me completely to himself. After our second daughter was born, all trust had been broken with their dad so when our baby turned 5 months old, we split up for good. There was no more turning back. I stopped going to church and I got into another relationship to find comfort for my shattered heart. Of course, nothing ever works out when JESUS isn't at the center.

SUMMARY

(Read Matthew 5:44) We must forgive those who hurt us and go a step further by blessing and praying for them. God wants us to keep our hearts pure. And although healing can be a process-confessing forgiveness should be instant. Forgiving others sets you free. When we hold on to the pain of the past it only makes us bitter and hinders us from blossoming into who we truly can be IN JESUS.

QUESTIONS – Chapter 6
1. How did you come to know God?

2. Did you ever believe in someone, only for them to hurt you once again?

3. Have you truly forgiven them?

4. Do you wish them well and pray for them?

5. Do you still find yourself talking about the same pain?

7

The Breakup

One of the pastors at a church I attended ended up reaching out to me when he found out I was going through a divorce and he asked me to come back to church. I was so embarrassed to return to church because I was going through a divorce and had a newborn baby. I felt like such a failure, but I had to be strong for my daughters.

Time went by and I got a little stronger. I joined the prayer partner team again and helped in the children's ministry. I even started to lead a singles group. I was finally feeling breakthrough and letting go of the pain of yesterday although I still needed a lot of healing. When I would minister to the children the volunteers would tell me "Patti we believe you have a gift to preach the gospel." I didn't see that at all. I could never see myself on a stage at church preaching although I had visions of it, and I knew deep inside God was calling me to preach. After all, God had been preparing me all along by giving me a zeal to study his word when I was just a baby Christian. I ended up leaving that church after 6 years because the pastor and I ended a 6-month relationship.

When things didn't work out, I no longer felt comfortable there. It was nothing against him. He was an amazing Pastor I just knew God was calling me elsewhere and I was right. I ended up meeting some Spanish pastors on Facebook who lived in my subdivision and we clicked immediately. Little did I know God was using that church to unlock the gift of preaching inside of me. The pastors loved me, and they allowed me to preach on Friday nights there. I also joined their Spanish worship team; however, when my oldest daughter had an ATV 4-wheeler accident and had to be life flighted to Memorial Hermann hospital...everything changed for me that day. I felt like an 18-wheeler truck hit my stomach when I heard the news. I was so anxious to see my daughter. I was in tears, but God gave me a supernatural peace. I had lots of support from friends, family, and pastors. The hospital was filled with many gifts and get-well cards. So many people were praying for me and my daughter. Praise God that HE healed my daughter in 1 month. She had 4 skull fractures and had to wear a neck brace. After her healing, my daughter wanted to attend an English-speaking church and it so happened that my friends from high school were starting a church. We started attending church there and it was so amazing. Both of my daughters loved it there. I got to preach to the youth there. I was a prayer partner, spoke at their outreach services and went out on the streets with their evangelical team. It was such an amazing experience.

SUMMARY

(Read Romans 8:28) God worked everything together for our good and God doesn't waste anything we go through. God's gifts are irrevocable. When God gives you a gift nothing or no one can take from you. What God has called you to no one can stop-no matter how many obstacles you have been through so be encouraged. You were born with a COMEBACK SPINE. NOTHING OR NO ONE CAN STOP YOUR DESTINY. So, it doesn't matter what you have been through-what matters is how you grow through it. REMEMBER-Nothing happens to you...it happens for you.

QUESTIONS – Chapter 7
1. Have you been through so much and have now experienced breakthrough? What does that feel like to you?

2. Through the pain-are you able to still see God unlock your gifts and show you what he has called you to do?
3. Did you know that there is purpose in your pain?

4. Have you ever gotten yourself in a relationship with an authority figure at church and things didn't work out?

5. If so, how did you handle the disappointment?

8

The Prophecy

Life was so good. I had finally found a church my girls and I loved. I had great friends there. Life couldn't get any better than that. I was a manager for a wonderful chiropractic firm, and I enjoyed working for the doctor. He was amazing. Everything was going great. By this time, I had a lot of Christian friends from different churches and I would attend different bible study groups at times. I would also attend women's conferences with my friends. I was on fire for God.

One afternoon in August of 2012, I went to a conference by my house with a friend and the lady who was speaking at the conference called me up to the front. She told me that I would be married by the end of the year of 2012. I didn't even have a boyfriend at the time, so I didn't know what to think. Everyone told me that she was such an amazing prophet, so I believed the prophesy. I didn't know how this was all going to happen, but I believed it.

A month later, I went to a bible study and I met a man there who had been my Facebook friend for about a year. We knew some of the same people. He was leading the bible study that night and he even prayed over me. I fell out right away under the power of the Holy Spirit. When this happens the power of God releases the presence of God in away sometimes that's more than your natural body can take. I was in awe of the anointing he carried.

He told me a shift was coming into my life. Little did I know he would be a huge part of that shift. We talked that night about all the wonderful things we both did in ministry. He even recorded me singing at the bible study since many asked me to sing that night. My friend loved his armor bearer. So, she kept insisting I talk to the minister. I didn't know what to think because of our age difference. I had never dated anyone 16 years older than myself. Although he was a mighty man of God, I somehow couldn't get over the fact that he was much older than I was. He invited me out to his revival to sing and I went along with my older daughter. We all went out to eat that night as a group and by this time I knew everyone was trying to get us together. They kept calling us the POWER COUPLE. Of course, I wanted a man of God since I was also in ministry, but I remember being very confused about this relationship.

At the time, I was a huge people pleaser and I wanted people's approval so being seen with a minister on his level was delightful; however, looking back I fell in love with the image rather than the person. The image of being married to a minister meant more to me than who I was marrying. Truth is, I was marrying a stranger who I was engaged to within 2 months of meeting. Everywhere we turned we got prophesies that we were supposed to be husband and wife. Coming out of all the darkness I had come out of…I felt a false sense of security marrying someone older than me who was also a minister. I believed he would never cheat on me and he would treat me and my girls with respect. However, I began to have doubts when I would test his heart concerning certain issues and he would get angry. I never had complete peace in marrying this man, but I did it anyway. We never went through any type of marital counseling. The pastors in our lives at the time trusted we were making the right decision.

He was rigid and restrictive. I loved to travel, he didn't. The age difference caused us not to have much in common. We argued a lot and just couldn't seem to see eye to eye on anything. He was set in his ways and not willing to change. He had distrust towards me and never shared what he brought into the household financially. He was kind to my girls, and he respected them. Our problems were ours. Why did I marry this man? Because as I mentioned earlier, I was a people pleaser, I wanted people's approval. I believed the prophesy and I felt secure initially with the image of being married to him.

SUMMARY

(Read Jeremiah 17:5-8) One thing I've learned the hard way is people will fail you, but God never will. We must be careful not to put our trust in people. We should always be in prayer when making decisions and not be led by anything else including a prophesy. If the prophecy does not align with Gods word, then we should question the word we received. Prophesy is only a confirmation of what God has already spoken or revealed to you.

QUESTIONS – Chapter 8
1. Have you ever made a bad decision out of being a people pleaser or wanting people's approval?

2. Have you ever done something not having a 100% peace about it only to end up regretting it?

3. Have you ever received a prophesy that turned your life upside down?

4. Have you ever gotten hurt by the church or a minister? Have you forgiven them?

5. Maybe you are a minister who hurt someone...have you apologized?

9

The Big Comeback

Who do you blame when a marriage only lasts 4 months? I would say both parties. I will take responsibility for my actions. I should have never married a stranger because of a prophecy. I thought that since we both loved JESUS, our relationship couldn't fail.

However, I found out that your relationships must be compatible, there must be some common ground outside of ministry. One should only marry out of LOVE and one should marry their best friend. You must build a strong foundation before ever thinking about marriage. I've heard people say, "Well I married my husband within 2 weeks of knowing him and we lasted forever." WELL GOOD FOR YOU. YOU'VE MET YOUR DESTINY.

We both had trust issues, and I couldn't see him leading our household. Truth is, he didn't trust me either. We didn't love each other. Our arguments began to be very unhealthy after a while. When he moved out, I filed for divorce after going to counseling with him for

6 months. Even in counseling we couldn't see eye to eye. When we started out, I never dreamed that the marriage would only last a few months.

I am thankful however for this experience as crazy as it sounds because I learned so much from it. God has taken the shattered pieces of everything I've gone through and he has put me back together STRONGER, BETTER AND WISER. I feel I can withstand any storm after all I've been through. I am not easily shaken. The main thing I regret is how this marriage affected my oldest daughter. My youngest was too young to realize what was happening. My oldest daughter walked with me through another divorce. She saw the tears and encouraged me to stay strong through this process. What hurt me the most was that I felt I failed God. There are always consequences for every good or bad decision we make. However, when you serve God, He causes all things to truly work together for your good and for His Glory.

When others thought that was the end of Patti, God said, "No Patti this is just the beginning." This divorce helped me deal with the issue of people pleasing. When we place the opinion of people above what we know to be true in our own hearts, we will always end up in a regrettable situation. I put myself in counseling acknowledging my wrongs. I sought out professional help because I wanted to get to the root of my problems. During this time, I focused on my relationship with God.

I listened to all the Godly counsel that was given to me. Second divorce and all, God didn't give up on me. I was loved by Him, and precious in His sight. I chased after God like never before, and this time, I surrendered everything to Him. I gave God all my broken pieces and He began to break me to share me with multitudes. I had no idea what God was up to at the time. The breaking didn't feel good, but I knew it was necessary. I was tired and had ran out of all options. All I had was God and He was all I ever really needed.

Once He was done with me in counseling, God put me at an amazing church with wonderful Pastors that just loved on me. Pastors Juan and Ruthy Martinez supported me through this process. They believed in me when I didn't believe in myself. They always spoke words of life and affirmation over me. Most importantly, they never judged me. They showed me the love of God at a time when I needed it most.

All I needed was LOVE. I didn't need anything else but God's love to wrap me in His Arms and that's exactly what HE did. Even the church is called "GET WRAPPED CHURCH". My Pastors trusted the call of God on my life, and God surrounded me with lots of baby Christians. He told me, "Patti, feed My sheep!" Every time I wanted to hold on to the pain like Peter, I could hear God saying to me again, "Patti do you love Me? I would say yes Lord I love you. "He would say feed my people."

The devil fought me long and hard. The Lord brought to my remembrance the revelation about the snake trying to bite me, how long it was, and how its head was cut off. The Lord said He chose me to cut the snakes' head off the generational curses of my bloodline.

You see God wasn't interested in my past failures. He was interested in my purpose. God knew I had wasted enough time making mistakes and beating myself up about them. It was time to take all the pain I went through and give it purpose. It was not easy. At times I wanted to sink in my pain and have a pity party, but destiny was calling my name!

SUMMARY

(Read Ephesians 1:11) Know that your pain has purpose. Moses was cast out into the wilderness after killing an Egyptian. It was not a fun place for him, but God used his pain and time in the wilderness to prepare him to lead the children of Israel out of Egypt and the wilderness. You can't take someone where you have never been. You must know the way. People need to hear your testimony so they can draw hope. They need to see you on the other side of your pain. They need to see you walk in your God given purpose. SO, share your story and give your pain wings to fly!

QUESTIONS – Chapter 9

1. Have you ever wanted to sink in your pain and stay there? What or who pulled you out?

2. Have you truly allowed God to give your pain a purpose?

3. Do you believe God has a plan for all the pain you have been through?
4. Have you found your purpose?

10

I Know Who I Am

I started leading the women's ministry and teaching the ladies bible studies at my church. I also created The Princess Closet event and the Once a Year Ladies Retreat in Galveston, Texas. God also allowed me to minister on radio. I wrote a post on Facebook about ministry, and TBN contacted me to come on to share my testimony. Since then, God has allowed me to see many women set free from the lies of the enemy. I now know that everything I went through had a purpose. I speak at different churches and God has placed an anointing upon my life to set the captives free. I am so honored to be a vessel that's useful for my Master. God has healed my broken heart. given me beauty for my ashes and the oil of JOY for my tears.

As I write this book, the process has been a positive journey that has caused me to be brave, and transparent. It has empowered me to speak my truth, and I would encourage others to do the same. My advice to anyone who reads this book is to NEVER give up. Do not quit. Storms will come against us, people won't always believe in us, but we must be our own greatest cheerleader. Don't wait for someone to encourage you, encourage yourself. Believe God for big things because we serve a BIG God. Don't put limits on Him. Chase after God with all that is within you, and watch God do amazing things in your life. Keep your heart pure and most of all, love God with all your heart, soul, and mind.

I am so excited about my future because God has promised to take me from faith to faith, victory to victory and from glory to glory. I know my best days are ahead of me and I'm ready to step into the greater destiny God has for me. My future looks so bright because God is in my tomorrow.

You too can have the same hope and faith I have by allowing God to become your everything. Tell God to use you and HE will use you for HIS GLORY. God has an amazing future ahead for you. Give HIM your pain, your failures, your sickness, your doubts, your insecurities, and HE will give you back SUCCESS, HEALING, FAITH, CONFIDENCE and PURPOSE. God is good and HE stands at the door of your heart ready for you to LET HIM IN so HE can dine with you and be your everything. If you've never accepted Jesus into your heart, tell Him right now. "Jesus, come into my heart, and be my Lord and Savior." Don't be afraid to talk to God. HE is your father, your husband, your best friend, your creator. God desires a relationship with you and if you already have a relationship with God know that God wants to take you DEEPER.

I always tell people that God is like an OCEAN and HE desires to take you DEEPER and DEEPER. Don't be afraid to surrender everything to God because HIS PLAN FOR YOUR LIFE IS BETTER THAN YOUR PLAN! Trust Him today and every day!

FINAL SUMMARY

(Read 1 Corinthians 2:9) In my own ability I could have never put myself on television, radio, lead women's ministry, speak at women's conferences, or even write a book. I didn't know I could do all this. It was God who has made me a loving mother today even though I didn't grow up with healthy love. It was God who gave me the creativity to do women events and be confident on national television and radio. It is God today who placed in my heart to write this book. When we surrender everything over to God...He will take over our lives and give us the ability to do anything! God is no respecter of people. HE is only a respecter of faith. So, what HE has done in my life HE desires to do in your life. I pray this book has stirred up your faith to believe God to do great things in your life, and you see the goodness of the LORD as you too choose to surrender everything over to God.

QUESTIONS – Chapter 10
1. Did you know that God has a better plan for you than you can ever plan for yourself?

2. Are you ready to trust God on a new level? If so, don't be afraid to step out in faith and do what God tells you to do.

3. If not, what keeps stopping you from giving God your everything?

It's Time

It's Time to Give GOD Everything
No More Holding Back Anything
It's Time to Forgive your Abuser
No More Chains, Its Time to Soar
It's Time to Release Your Broken Pieces
And Give Them All to JESUS
It's Time to Break Free
And Walk in Your New Identity
It's Time to Let Go of All the Lies
Look Up, Now is the Time to Rise
No More Staying Parked in Your Pain
And Rehearsing the Loss, Only the Gain
It's Time to Enjoy the Abundant Life
JESUS gave You when HE Died
On the Cross at Calvary
So, you can Know HIS Peace
JESUS is Cheering You On
From HIS Mighty Throne
So Now is the Time, Not Tomorrow
Today, you can Let Go of Your Sorrow
And Experience HIS Amazing Grace
It's Time to Solely Focus on Your Race
That was Set before You Called Destiny
And Go where You have Never Been
Deeper into GODs Ocean
And Let Your Soul be Made Clean
It's Time to Let Go of What is Shattered
And Surrender it All to the ONE Who Always
Mattered